HYDRA

today and yesterday

ΕΚΔΟΣΕΙΣ
ΤΕΧΝΗ
EDITIONS

ATHENS 2004

*Previous page: The statue
of the Hydraiot Admiral and
leader of the Greek War
of Independence
Andreas Miaoulis,
at the entrance
of the port.*

*On the right: The town
and the port of Hydra.*

© Copyright 2004   MICHAEL TOUBIS PUBLICATIONS S.A.
                     Nisiza Karela, Koropi, Attiki.
                     Telephone: +30 210 6029974, Fax: +30 210 6646856
                     Web Site: http://www.toubis.gr

ISBN: 960-540-455-9

Hydra, *wood carving by K. Grammatopoulos, 90 x 120 cm., 1980.*

CONTENTS

View of the west side of the port.

The islands of the Argolic and Saronic Gulfs
are priceless jewels, gracing both gulfs
with their bountiful beauty.
The Athenians are lucky that they can reach these
islands in such a short time, far from the noisy city.
Three of the five largest islands of the Argosaronic –
Salamis, Aegina and Poros – are located within
the Saronic Gulf, the gulf between the coasts
of Attica and the Peloponnese.
There is a rich ancient Greek mythology relating
to these islands, and the mythology of the gulf that
surrounds them is just as abundant.
It is said that it took its name from Saron, the King
of ancient Troezen in the Peloponnese, opposite Poros.
Once when hunting a deer, Saron fell into the sea and
drowned. From then on the gulf was named the Saronic.
Hydra, along with the island of Dokos
which is today uninhabited, is situated between
the Saronic and the Argolic Gulfs.
The Argolic Gulf took its name from
the historic city of Argos, which is near Nafplion.
In this guide we will introduce you to the
beautiful island of Hydra.

Hydra

The noble lady of the Argosaronic

ydra's fame has spread beyond the borders of Greece, reaching as far as the other side of the world. All visitors to the island talk of the pretty harbour with the traditional houses built spread over the rocky slopes of the surrounding hills. Of the wonderful mansions built in grey stone with a white outline around the windows, the mansions built by the Hydraiot captains with much love, when their merchant fleet ruled the whole of the Mediterranean and brought great wealth to the island. In the days when little Hydra flourished and was indeed the noble lady of the Argosaronic.

This economic prosperity was to be cut off by the Greek Revolution of 1821 against the Turks. The Hydraiots, who loved freedom more than wealth and grandeur, threw themselves into the Struggle with a passion. They transformed their commercial ships into battleships, arming them with cannons, and, along with the Spetsiots and Psarians, successfully fought the Turkish fleet. At the head of the Greek fleet, the idol of the Hydraiots until today even, was their compatriot Andreas Miaoulis.

The war lasted for seven whole years, and the miracle came in the end. Greece had managed to defeat a whole empire and free itself. Little Hydra and its ships had played a decisive role in this struggle.

The price of victory was, however, ultimately very heavy for the Hydraiots. They had used up all their wealth for the Struggle, and most of their ships had been destroyed. It seemed that the game was finally up, and the Hydraiots began to abandon their barren island. Then there was another miracle, and this time *The cosmopolitan* without a war, without a fleet and without cannons. *port of Hydra.* In the 1950s, artists and intellectuals from Greece

and abroad began to congregate on the island and immortalise its charms with their pens and with their paint brushes. The intellectuals were followed by the tourists, whose number was constantly on the rise. Within a few years, then, the island had evolved into an intellectual and artistic centre, and Hydra again became the noble lady of the Argosaronic.

Geography

Hydra is located between the Saronic and the Argolic Gulfs, at a distance of four to five miles from the Peloponnesian coast. It is long and narrow, with a length of around 18 kilometres and a broadest width of 5 km. It has a surface area of 50 kilometres and a coastline of 55 km.

The island has about 2600 permanent residents, in contrast with the summer months, when this figure increases greatly. There are daily connections with Piraeus, which is 37 nautical miles away.

Morphology

In contrast with many of the Argosaronic islands, Hydra is for the most part bare and rocky with pine trees only in its south-west section. The highest mountain, Eros (590 m.), is located in the centre of the island, to the south of Hydra town.

There are a few small bays in its northern coasts, such as Mantraki, the port of Hydra, and Ayios Georgios at Bisti. There are two larger bays in the southern coast, Ayios Nikolaos and Limnionizas. As for the valleys, the main one is that at Episkopi in the southern part of the island.

The islet of Dokos

This islet, lying in between Hydra and the Peloponnesian coast, was for the Hydraiots the main source of the beautiful grey stone with which they built most of their houses and mansions. There was a quarry in operation here many years ago in order to mine the stone. The islet, which is bare and rocky on its southern side, has a surface area of 13 square kilometres. According to the 2001 census, Dokos has 43 habitants.

Research has shown that this islet was inhabited from the Bronze Age, 6,000 years ago. Finds from this period have been uncovered along the whole length of the coast. In 1975 the earliest known shipwreck, dating from 2,500-2,000 BC, was found in the bed of Cape Skintos. Underwater excavations in 1989-1992 recovered stone tools, anchors, clay pots, vases and other vessels. These finds are on exhibit in the Spetses Museum.

The island's strategic position appears to have inspired the Byzantines, under either Heraclius or Constantine IV, into building a castle on the east side

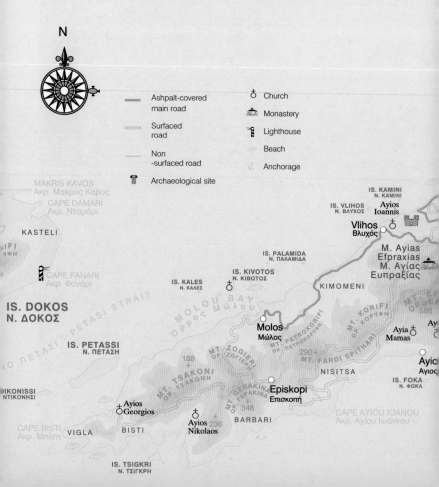

in the 7th century AD. This castle must have been built in combination with the castle of Monemvasia and the castle of Thermisios Hermione, and was also used by the Venetians. The castle fortifications, facing the north side of the island, covered a large area, indicating that the island had a significant population during this period.

Outside the castle are the remains of two churches, one built in the basilica style.

The north beach of Dokos is today a favourite spot for trips and camping. There is a nunnery on the island.

Historical

History of Hydra

View of the town of Hydra.
Thomas Hope, 1795.

*O*n ancient times the island was known as Hydrea. This is how the great ancient historians Hecataeus and Herodotus referred to it. Heysichius of Alexandria was the first to call it 'Hydra' in his *Lexicon*. The Venetians called the island Sidra, and only in 1768 is it again referred to as Hydra, by Lozie in his *'History of the Venetian Republic.'*

Hydra was occupied in the Mycenean period.

Introduction

This is apparent from the excavations conducted to the south-west of the town, in the region of Vlychos. Any earlier periods of occupation would have been for a short duration and took place when the island was used as a way station between the Peloponnese and the Cyclades. The Dryopes appear to have been the first race to pass through Hydra and settle here permanently. They were a mountain people who lived

around the mountains of Oitis and Parnassos, and who were later displaced by the Dorians. The Dryopes were able, more than any other peoples, to face the difficult conditions on the island and partake, as in their original homeland, in animal husbandry.

Around two or so centuries after the arrival of the Dryopes, dated to the 13th century BC, the Dorians descended, marking thus the end of the Mycenean period on Hydra.

In his reference to Hydrea, Herodotus writes that in the 6th century BC fugitives from Samos who had unsuccessfully attempted to overthrow the tyrant Polykrates, were sailing around on the Aegean and disembarked at Siphnos, the island that was rich in gold mines. Here, they violently grabbed 100 talents and, with this money, purchased Hydra from the inhabitants of Hermione on the Peloponnese opposite, to whom the island then belonged. The Samians later sold Hydra to the Troezens, the inhabitants of the then powerful city to the north,

Map of Hydra, *by an anonymous artist. Engraving, 15x18.5 cm, 1584.*

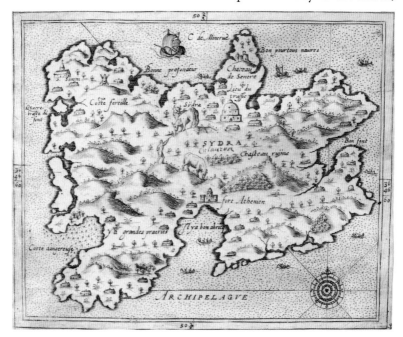

opposite Poros, under whose control it remained until the 4th century BC.

We do not have any information on the island for the classical period, aside from a reference by the historian and geographer Stephanus Byzantius, who mentions that there was a shepherd named Evagis on the island who was also a comic playwright. Only a few details survive for the periods of Macedonian and Roman rule and for the long Byzantine period. This fact has led to the conviction that Hydra was unoccupied during these years, something which is not completely accurate. The truth is that the constant pirate raids forced a large number of the population to abandon the island, whilst the rest distanced themselves from the coasts and dispersed around the hinterland. We are led to this conclusion by the fact that many bronze and gold Byzantine coins have been found at the Bishopric, as well as evidence for occupation during much earlier periods.

The Byzantine period on the island ended in 1204 with the coming of Venetian rule. The subsequent war between the Venetians and the Turks led to the island coming under Turkish rule, although this did not result in any changes to the demographic problem.

The obscurity and apparent desertion of Hydra was ended in around 1470 by the Arvanites Orthodox Christians who passed over to the island from the Peloponnese to escape Turkish persecution. These Arvanites were the descendants of those whom the Despots of Mystra, Kantakouzenos and Palaiologos had invited to settle in their region, in order to increase the falling population of the Peloponnese. The new settlers on Hydra merged with the old, and together they began anew to build the first houses of the town on the hill of Kiafas, and to throw themselves into the struggle for survival. The dry and barren land of the island forced them to turn to the sea. The beginning was made with the building of small ships, for them to proceed a little later - in the mid-18th century - to building larger ones. Shortly before the end of the 18th century, the Hydraiots had 150 large merchant ships in their possession. It was clear that with such a fleet, Hydra could achieve much in the fields of commerce and shipping, as indeed happened. The island was of course helped in this direction by other events and coincidences.

As for relations with ruling Turkey, Hydra enjoyed quite a few privileges. The island was governed by local Hydraiot notables and a Turkish representative, who was appointed by the Hydraiots themselves. Two wars took place during the period of Turkish rule which were exceptionally favourable to the Hydraiots. The first was the war between Russia and Turkey (1768-1774), which ended with Turkey's defeat and the signing of the Treaty of Kutchuk Kaynarca, by which the Bosphorus strait was opened, meaning that Hydraiot ships could now sail through to the Black Sea and supply the Mediterranean with wheat.

The second war was that against Napoleon during which the British blockaded the Mediterranean. The courageous Hydraiots, however, were brave enough to break through the blockade and thus control all shipping through the Mediterranean.

An important factor in the island's economic growth was the reform of the system of government in 1802 and the appointment of G. Voulgaris, who was favoured by the Turks, as Governor of the island. During this period the Hydraiots built many boats, greatly strengthened the merchant navy, constructed elegant mansions, founded a naval school and built schools and churches. This was when Ibrahim Pasha, the Ottoman Commander-in-Chief, described Hydra as a 'Little England.'

These excellent captains would unload their goods in the west and return loaded with luxurious furniture, porcelains and paintings from Italy and France and, of course, with lots of money, so that Hydra became the wealthiest region of Greece. The

The Ascension
of Christ,
*wall painting
from the
Monastery
of Agios Nikolaos,
17th century.*

large mansions in grey stone were built under the supervision of Italian craftsmen and were furnished according to western prototypes. Naturally, this wealth also led to social progress and many functions and balls were organised in special halls, at which foreign orchestras performed.

The captains and the people of Hydra may have loved all this luxury and wealth. Yet, there was something which for them had even more significance: their love of freedom. The hour for the uprising against the Turks had arrived. The Peloponnesian opposite had already risen, and now they were inviting the Hydraiots, who had power, to help them. The notables at first hesitated, but the people were not to be restrained. They revoked the Turkish representative and appointed Antonios Oikonomos to be their own governor. The notables agreed to this and Hydra finally took its part in the Revolution of 1821. Yet, the island was not alone. Alongside it were another two islands which contributed their fleets to the Struggle: neighbouring Spetses and distant Psara.

The leader of the collective fleet was the Hydraiot Admiral Andreas Miaoulis. Next to him were brave fighters, such as Voulgaris, Tobazis, Sachtouris, Tsamados, etc. Their achievements became known throughout the whole of Europe.

The merchant ships, which were armed and converted into battle ships, brought fear to the Turks. Their fireships - small ships loaded with explosives, which slid around in the dark and even dared to enter the Turkish ports and blow up the battle ships - became legendary.

The Struggle lasted for a whole seven years, and in the end the Greeks won and Greece was

liberated. Hydra and the other two islands were among the major contributors to this victory. Yet, the Hydraiots had given their all: their ships, money and barren land could no longer support them. In the mid-19th century they were forced to turn to sponge diving, which unfortunately declined after a few years, along with the island. Most of the sailors gradually began to abandon the island, and it took a great painter, Hadjikyriakos Gikas, to appear on the island in the 1950s, and for many films with internationally-renowned stars to be made here, for the island to begin to live again and finally to become an international tourist centre.

In the interior of the Cathedral of Hydra, one can see the Greek flag along with the gonfalon of Hydra, Holy Symbol of the Greek War of Independence.

THE LEADERS OF THE GREEK WAR OF INDEPENDENCE IN HYDRA

Andreas Miaoulis
(Phila, Euboea, 1796 - Athens, 1835)

*A*ndreas Miaoulis was active in shipping from his youth. He made much profit from maritime trade, which enabled him to purchase ships with large capacities. He was declared Admiral of the Hydraiots in late 1821. His first gallant deed was participating in the naval battle of Patras on 20/2/1822. He subsequently distinguished himself at Chios, Nafplio, Psara and at the naval battle of Gerontas (1824), the largest maritime conflict during the Greek War of Independence. He attempted to avert Ibrahim from landing in the Peloponnese (1825) and to reinforce Messolonghi during its second siege. Capodistirias was especially impressed by him and made him leader of the Aegean fleet.

Miaoulis, however, was one of the leaders of the movement against Capodistirias, even reaching the point of ordering the firing of the Greek ships in the port of Poros, an act that besmirched his name. He was appointed to the committee that visited Munich to offer the loyalty of the Greek nation to Otto, who subsequently appointed him leader of the Naval Department and general supervisor of the fleet. He died in Athens and was buried at Piraeus, along the coast (akti) that is today known as Akti Miaoulis.

Georgios Sahtouris
(Hydra, 1783-1841)

A leading figure in the of the naval battles of the War of Independence, Georgios Sahtouris was Vice Admiral of the Hydraiot fleet and one of the bravest fighters during naval operations. He fought for the liberation of Chios and in the attempts to recapture the island of Psara after its destruction in 1824. His counsel was decisive during the naval battles of Mykale, Gerontas and Kaferea. He took part in providing supplies to the besieged at Messolonghi (1826) and in the efforts to fire the Egyptian fleet at Alexandria (1827). Capodistrias appointed him head of the fleet along the coast of Messene, with responsibility for blockading the seas in the area of Ambrakiko to Crete. During King Otto's reign he was governor of the naval war station at Poros.

Georgios Voulgaris
(1758 - 1812)

The "Bey" of the Hydraiots. He served in the Turkish fleet and in 1802 became the island's Governor. Favoured by the Turks, he laid the foundations for the development of the merchant navy and the peaceful daily life of the Hydraiots, without the presence of the Turks.

Georgios Kountouriotis
(Hydra, 1782 - 1858)

Georgios Koutouriotis was an important figure of the Greek War of Independence. He took part in the 2nd National Council at Astros and was appointed president of the Executive Committee in December 1823. In 1825 he was given command of the attacks against Ibrahim but was subsequently forced to quit as he was unable to complete the task successfully. In 1837 King Otto appointed him Vice President of the State Council and, in 1843, President of the Senate. In 1848 he formed a government. He was not, however, able to challenge the internal and external problems and was replaced by the government of Constantine Kanaris. He died having remained loyal to King Otto to his final days.

Iakovos Tobazis (Yiakoumakis)
(Hydra, 1722 - 1829)

Tobazis was active in shipping from his youth, and quickly became a ship owner. In 1818, he was initiated into the Friendly Society and was heavily involved in the preparations for the War of Independence. With the outbreak of the War, he gave his ships over to the service of the Revolution. He took part in the naval campaign of Chios and in the northeast Aegean. The Turkish fleet was very strong and the challenge difficult. It was thus decided to use fire ships, and it was later said that Tobazis had proposed this idea. He directed the firing of the Turkish frigate at Eressos under Papanicholas. He was active in the sea around Samos, as well as the southern and western coasts of the Peloponnese. In addition to his boats, Tobazis also gave over all his wealth to the cause of the Revolution.

Lazaros Kountouriotis
(Hydra, 1769 - 1852)

An important political figure of the 1821 War of Independence, and one of its principle financial backers, especially during the first period. He was appointed a Senator by King Otto.

Anastasios Tsamados
(Hydra, 1774 - Sphactiria, 1825)

*T*samados was active in shipping and, on the outbreak of the War of Independence, he transformed his ship into a warship. In 1821, as part of the Hydraiot fleet, he took part in the operations in the Aegean and at Pagasitiko. During the following years he took part in almost all the naval campaigns in the Aegean, along the Peloponnesian coast and the Corinth gulf. In 1825 he put into port at Neokastro with food and military supplies and successfully sent provisions to the fortress that was under siege by Ibrahim. Tsamados was killed at Sphactria during the attack by Ibrahim's troops.

Georgios Sahinis
(Hydra, 1789 - Athens, 1864)

*G*eorgios Sahinis was one of the most able captains of the Greek fleet during the 1821 War of Independence. He was educated in Corfu and was active in shipping from a young age. With the outbreak of the War he joined the Hydraiot fleet under the command of Miaoulis. He took part in many naval campaigns and his language skills meant that on many occasions he was put to good use by the Greek government for negotiations with the enemy fleet or the fleets of the foreign powers. In 1823 he was made governor Syros and Mykonos and in 1836 was appointed head of the Aegean fleet. He was a guard of honour to King Otto and director of the Naval Directorate of the Poros.

Antonios Oikonomou
(Hydra, 1785 – Koutsopodi, Argos, 1821)

A leading figure of the Revolution of March 1821, he took over the Government House along with the sailors and forced the nobles to participate in the Struggle, to which they had initially reacted against. As a result of the power that he had acquired, he later came into conflict with the wealthy Hydraiots, who had him killed in December 1821.

Antonios Kriezis
(Troezen, 1796 – Athens, 1865)

*M*ember of a leading shipping family. He was in disagreement with Antonios Oikonomou when the Revolution broke out in Hydra. Later, however, he participated in all the campaigns of the Hydraiot fleet. He was Commander of the fleet of Western Greece under Governor Capodistrias, and he was also part of King Otto's close circle. He retired from politics in 1854, after having served in the highest public positions (as a Minister and Prime Minister).

Yesterday and today

Replica of Ares,
the legendary 'briki'
boat of the
Greek Revolution
that belonged
to Tsamados.

People and Occupations

Shipping was a beloved activity of the Hydraiots since the old days, and there is much sadness among the people of the island that they are no longer able to live from the sea. Lefteris Grypaios, for example, is the last of the shipbuilders, a tradition dating from the people who "built" the boats of Miaoulis, the Admiral of the 1821 War of Independence. In 1991, Gryparis was forced to abandon shipbuilding, as a result of the tourist industry, limiting himself to a small workshop where he creates wonderful miniature ships.

Work in the tourist sector has, in the case of Hydra, led to the decline of the old ships, the old occupations, but has, however, definitely created new jobs for the locals. Small, elegant tourist accommodations, restaurants, cafes, and diving schools are always ready, especially during the summer period, to offer the island's visitors high-quality services.

Hydraiots are known for their love for the sea and their respect for tradition.

**Customs
& Traditions
Traditional
costumes**

The Hydraiots may have lived through tumultuous times. A tough struggle for survival when they first settled on the island, later struggles on the sea and at war. Yet, this did not prevent them from expressing their religious faith at every opportunity and of preserving their local customs. The 150 churches and 7 monasteries on Hydra, an island with a relatively small population, demonstrate the islanders' religious faith.

As for the local customs, many of these are fading or have disappeared altogether. There are, however, some which are maintained until our days. The most important of these is the **wedding**. In the old days, the Hydraiot wedding included features which we do not encounter on any other islands. We will not go into details about the 'making of the bed', which continues to take place throughout the whole of Greece. This is when guests and relatives offer their gifts to the couple-to-be by placing them on the bridal bed. We should, however, mention the 'washing of the bride's hair', which is done on the Saturday, the day before the wedding, by two married women who themselves have successful marriages. These same women must 'brush the bride's hair' on the Sunday morning before the wedding. Also characteristic is the gesture by the father of the bride towards his daughter at the door of the house, when he gives her a pouch containing gold coins or jewellery before the whole family leaves for the church.

The bride would wear the traditional formal wedding dress, on which stood out the 'kontogouni' (a short pelisse) made of silk velvet with gold embroidery which they called the 'yianniotiko,' and the 'tsemperi,' an embroidered headscarf which was also made of silk. The tsemperi meant that the women could not wear a necklace, but they wore instead a gold pin, the 'lalana,' over their breast. The bride and the groom would meet in the church. If the groom was a notable, then once the service was completed he would remove the tsemperi from the bride, and replace it with a fez with a golden tassel and kiss her.

The wedding banquet was held at lunch-time, whilst the celebration for friends took place in the evening, with much song and dance to the accompaniment of local instruments which then, as now, were the violin and the lute:

In Votsi's garden,
the lute and the violin sing.

The custom which most surprises, however, is that of the **Epitaphios**, the Good Friday funeral procession of Christ, at Kamini. At this village, the Epi-

Left page:
Traditional
costume from
the Museum
of Hydra.

Below:
Funeral
procession
of Christ,
at Camini
(PHOTO HYDRA
«GLIKAS»).

taphios proceeds into the sea, in an invocation to Christ to keep the waters calm and so help the sailors. The common custom of the burning of the effigy of Judas takes place on the night of the Resurrection.

The **New Year's customs** on Hydra are of especial interest. The doors of the house remain open from the morning, as the head of the household awaits the first visitor who will pass over the threshold uninvited. He will then hang a gift around the visitor's neck with a lace and they will have lunch together. If the head of the household just happens to be a notable, then the lucky visitor will surely receive the gift of a gold florin.

Festivals
Cultural
Events

The following **festivals** take place on Hydra: on 20 August at the Monastery of the Profitis Ilias, on 25 July at the Monastery of Ayia Evpraxia, on 25 March at the Monastery by the port, and on 14 November at Ayios Konstantinos the Hydraiot at Kiafa.

The **Miaoulia** festival takes place on the nearest weekend to 21 June each year in honour of the Hydraiot Admiral and hero of the Revolution of 1821 Andreas Miaoulis. It lasts for three days, and includes boat races, swimming competitions, dance, etc. On the last day there is a reconstruction of the firing of the Turkish flagship with Bengal lights, and food and drink on offer.

On **Carnival Sunday**, the famous Hydra carnival traverses the lanes of the island, filled with a large crowd of masked revellers. Every July the **International Puppet Festival** is held, under the aegis of the Municipality of Hydra and the Ministry of Culture. This is a non-profit making collaboration between Greece and Sweden.

Left:
The Miaoulia
festival
(PHOTO HYDRA
«GLIKAS»).

The **"Kountourioteia"** Folk Dance Festival also takes place in August, with yachting competitions in March and October. Finally, important cultural events, such as concerts and art exhibitions, are held in the Melina Mercouri **Art and Concert Hall.**

Below:
The Carnival of
Hydra.
(PHOTO HYDRA
«GLIKAS»).

Local cuisine

Since we are talking about food, let's say a couple of words about the local cuisine. The almonds of Hydra are widely celebrated, as are the pears served with a co-loured bow and cloves.

The sugar baklava is another popular desert of a thinlaye-red pastry with wal-nuts and syrup. As for the food, we note the pasta and myzithra (a soft cheese) dish, and the 'boubari' (stomach filled with rice, mince and spices and baked in the oven).

Arts and Letters

The Hydra of yesterday was the island of the captains, the heroes and the politicians. This little island has given Greece five prime ministers and around fifty government ministers. Today it is the island of the people of the arts and letters. Yet, the roots of these people are, of course, located in yesterday, when great figures, such as the historian Georgios Kriazis, Andreas Miaoulis, the historian, folklorist and member of the Athens Academy A. Lignos, the historian and folklorist A. Manikis, the professors of ophthalmology Spilios Haramis and I. Haramis, and many others lived.

And yet today, the list of Hydraiot intellectuals and artists who, along with their distinguished colleagues, lived and live on the island is still long. Among them, we find great artists, writers, academics and Nobel prize winners: Hadjikyriakos Gikas, Vyzantios, George Seferis, Odysseus Elytis, Petsalis, Pikionis, Henry Miller, Patrick Leigh Fermor and, last but not least, Leonard Cohen. The cultural and intellectual revival which can be observed on the island, along with its magic and charm, have made Hydra one of the leading international tourist spots.'

LEADING ARTISTS
OF HYDRA

Nikos Hadjikyriakos-Gikas
(Athens 1906 - 1994)

*H*e played a leading role in the flourishing of the arts on Hydra. A sculptor and painter, he studied in Paris and worked alongside Parthenis. Επηρεάστηκε έντονα από τα σύγχρονα ρεύματα και ιδιαίτερα από τον κυβισμό. He represented Greece at many international exhibitions, whilst in 1972 he was elected a member of the Athens Academy and in 1986 an honorary member of the Royal Academy of London.

Panayiotis Tetsis
(Athens 1925)

*P*anayiotis Tetsis studied in Paris and came under the influence of Pikionis and Hadjikyriakos-Gikas. He taught at the Higher School of Fine Arts from 1977, and in 1993 was elected a member of the Athens Academy.

Pericles Vyzantios
(Athens 1893 - 1972)

A painter, director and cartoonist. His beloved island of Hydra, where he spent the last 20 years of his life, features in many of his works. He was active in the foundation of the School of Fine Arts on Hydra, and was its Director for many years.

Works by him are on exhibition in the mansion of Lazaros Kountouriotis. He is well known for his landscapes and his late works consist studies of the Greek sunlight.

Constantine Vyzantios
(Athens 1924)

A painter and engraver. He studied in Paris and worked alongside his father, Pericles Vyzantios. Works by him are on exhibition in the mansion of Lazaros Kountouriotis.

Demetrios Pikionis
(Piraeus 1887 - 1968)

*D*emetrios Pikionis, a painter and engineer, studied at the School of Civil Engineering of the National Polytechnic University, followed by free drawing and sculpture in Munich and finally painting and architectural composition in Paris. He is regarded as a leading figure of Greek architecture, with a strong influence on the field. Pikionis experimented with new forms, incorporating into his creative output folk tradition and various periods of Greek history. He was appointed associate professor of Decoration at the Architecture School of the National Polytechnic University in 1925 and full professor in 1945. In 1966 he was elected a member of the Athens Academy, to the chair in Architecture.

Their first houses were nothing more than wooden huts and their first ships simple wooden hulls. Slowly, slowly, they began to use stone, whilst some, who had come from the slave galleys of Egypt taught them the craft of shipbuilding using wood, and they began to build real ships.

The first stone houses appeared at Kiafa, the rocky hill to the south of the port, which, with its steep slopes and its surrounding streams provided safety. With these, they created a defensive settlement, with tall walls, narrow lanes and covered walkways. This kind of architecture was a combination of the styles found on the Aegean islands and on the mainland. Unfortunately, the whole of the settlement was destroyed, and only three of its churches remain today. The Hydraiots rebuilt their settlement though, preserving many of the elements of the old, whilst also gradually expanding their town towards the port, and a little later, towards today's Kaminia and Vlycho.

The materials they used were stone and wood, which they acquired primarily from the neighbouring islet of Dokos. In order to build with stone, they used a mortar made from clay, known as 'kokkina,' to which they later added straw and limestone. For the mansions, this mortar was called 'koursani' and was enriched with sand, ground tiles, and an earth known as 'pitreliana.' Wood was used to 'bind' the ordinary houses, whilst in the mansions they used iron. Wood was, however, necessary in both types of houses for the construction of the roof, the 'liakos,' as they called it. For this, they used the trunks of mainly cypress trees, laying them out side-by-side a little apart one from the other. Over the trunks they added a layer of thin branches of planks, seaweed, 'kokkina,' a layer of earth around 30 cm. thick, and a layer of earth mixed with clay and limestone. On top of all this they placed the tiles. The final layer was of mortar, so as to ensure dryness. The 'liakos' was later covered with ceramic tiles, and few houses today still have their original structure.

Architecture

The mansion of Emmanouil Tobazis.

The earliest houses consisted of just one orthogonal room, and the auxiliary areas were detached, just as happens in farmhouses today. This house design evolved by adding other rooms on one or more floors. These rooms were adjoining and had the same arrangement. The larger houses were built in the shape of an L or a had wings on both sides. The exterior was simple. There was one external stone staircase, and usually a wooden staircase inside. The interior of the house was divided into the 'andres' (men's) or 'good salon,' the bedrooms, kitchen, oven, storeroom and bathroom. There was a yard with tall walls, quite a bit of vegetation, and the essential cistern for water storage. In some cases, there is a shop on the ground floor or a lounge and kitchen. For the facade, the white of the limestone initially predominated. Later, they began to use ochra or even stronger colours. The same happened with the door and window frames, which were at first painted in a light grey or green, and later in far more vibrant colours.

As for the mansions, these kept many of the features of the ordinary houses. That which made them stand apart, however, was the size and luxury of the interior. Indeed, most of these mansions had been built by Italian artisans who had been invited over for this purpose. Another characteristic is the white outline around the windows, which breaks up the monotone grey of the building. Inside, the mansions are roomy with tall ceilings. In addition to the standard rooms, there was often a room in which to smoke a narghile (a water-pipe), and a smaller room with an icon stand. The luxurious furniture, brought over from west and east, is impressive.

All this wealth, which had accumulated on the island by the early 19th century, was the product of a collective effort on the part of the Hydraiot captains and their men. With their courage and strengths they succeeded in making their merchant fleet rule the Mediterranean waves, even breaking through the blockade imposed by the British.

A story which is told of an unexpected meeting

Images of traditional architecture.

between the then young Andreas Miaoulis, future admiral of the Greek fleet, with the British admiral Nelson is revealing. Miaoulis had been arrested for infringing the British blockade, an act punishable by death. The British admiral, full of curiosity, asked to see this brave young man. When Nelson saw Miaoulis standing bravely before him, he asked him "What would you do if you were in my position?" To which Miaoulis, undaunted, answered, "I would hang you." At which Nelson did not simply allow him to live, but he freed him.

Images of traditional architecture.

The port

of Hydra

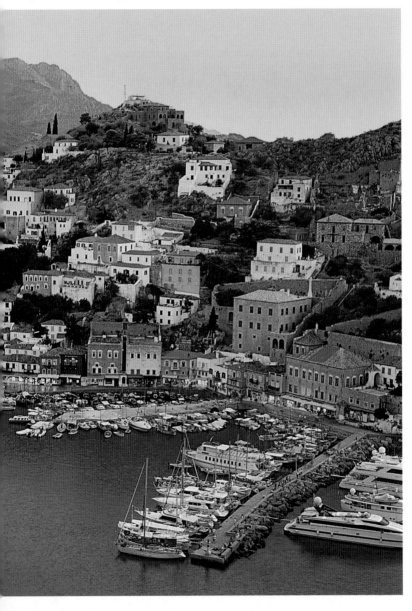

Tour
of the port

*T*he traveller visiting the Argosaronic for the first time is impatient to glimpse a sight of the celebrated Hydra. Yet, as the boat begins to approach the bare island, not much of a great impression is at first made. But suddenly, just before entering the port, something miraculous happens! All that the visitor has seen and heard up until this point pales into insignificance in front of the reality.

A closed bay, with rocky hills all around it and mountains behind, stands before him. The town is built spread out on all sides over the rocks, a town the like of which he has never seen before. Two- and three-storey houses, all built in grey stone, following an austere, frugal design. They look like giant cubes with tiles or a roof for the lid. There is almost no external decoration, the only exception being the white cornice around the door and window frames,

Panoramic view of the town of Hydra.

which somewhat dissipates the monotony of the grey. Some of the houses stand out because of their size: these are the famed mansions of the captains, decorating the town. All around the quay are countless colourful boats, small and large, which add their own note to this magical picture.

Before entering the port, the boat turns before the east cannon station which, as with the one in the west opposite, protected the entrance to the port during the years of the War of Independence against the Turkish yoke. There, within a raised square, is a bronze statue of the Hydraiot admiral and leader of the Struggle Andreas Miaoulis, who, despite the years which have passed, remains the idol of the Hydraiots. The admiral wears his military naval outfit

1

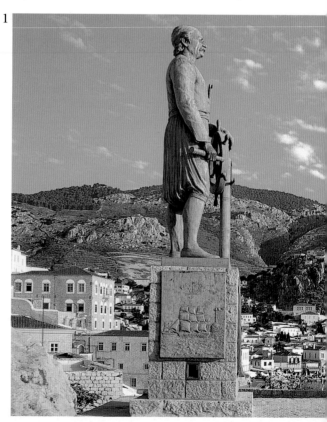

and holds onto the wheel of a battle ship. The road beneath the square leads to the organised beach of Mantraki. From here the visitor who wishes to go for a walk along the port of Hydra will encounter, whilst strolling along the length of the waterfront in the direction of the town centre, two large, identical buildings, the second of which is home to the port authority.

2

1. The statue of the Hydraiot admiral Andreas Miaoulis, at the entrance of the port.
2. The entrance of the port with the cannon station.

The Historical Archive and Museum of Hydra.

The beautiful, two-storey building a little further down is the **Historical Archive and Museum of Hydra** which was founded in 1918. Amongst the Archives are important documents which highlight Hydra's leading role, in the 18th and 19th century, in particular the period of the 1821 Greek War of Independence. The Museum has exhibits of relics from the Balkan Wars, the First and Second World Wars, a wonderful picture gallery, the arms of Hydraiot Independence fighters, and much more, bringing the whole of the island's heroic past to life within its walls. The Library holds 5,500 volumes, mainly of old editions that date to the early 18th century and 18,000 original documents of the Community of Hydra (1708-1865) and other material. The Museum also hosts many cultural events in its specially designed Rooms.

A few metres past the Historical Archive to the left are some three-storey mansions, including the **mansion of Tsamados**. A little to the south, at the en-trance to the middle of the port area and opposite the breakwater is the dock at which the boats and the speedboats moor. There is a lot of movement at this point, as might be expected, and the tables belonging to the row of cafes here are always full.

View of the town from the south-east. The Metropolitan church of Hydra can be seen, with its two belfries.

View of the town and the port of Hydra.

1

*1. The Cathedral of Hydra.
2. The grave of Lazaros Kountouriotis in the Cathedral.*

In the south-east corner of the port the 'sea taxis', as they are called, are always ready to take travellers to the other coasts of the island. These are small speedboats, adapted in such a way so as to be able to travel even when there is a strong meltemi wind. All these boats have a couple of little flags at their sides: the Greek flag and the flag that was used on the island during the War of Independence, with the cross and the slogan "Eleftheria i Thanatos" (freedom or death). This flag does not appear just on the sea taxis, but also on the public buildings. Over 175 years have passed since the Revolution, but it appears that the Hydraiots, just like the Spetsiots, want to keep these memories alive.

From the 'taxi' corner, the waterfront turns to the west. This is the most central section, with banks, shops, restaurants and cafes. There are quite a lot of people here, especially at nights, that the lights create a phantasmagoric atmosphere. Some people are taking a stroll, whilst others are sitting at the tables.

The **Monastiri**, as the Metropolitan church of Hydra is called, is located some-where in the middle of the coastal road. It was built in the mid-17th century as the cathedral church of a monastery. It is a three-aisled domed basilica, the aisles of which are separated by rows of columns. The central aisle is dedicated to the Dormition of the Virgin, and the church celebrates its feast day on 15 August. The decoration in its interior is rich. The two marble belfries, one of which also has a clock, are impressive.

Amongst the graves in the forecourt of the church is that of Lazaros Kountouriotis, a patron of the War of 1821, whilst an **Ecclesiastical Museum** has been opened up in a special hall developed in the section of the monks' cells around the monastery.

2

The coastal road becomes quite wide at the point in front of the Metropolitan church, creating a three-cornered square. This is the **square of Pavlos Kountouriotis**, and a grand marble statue of him stands in its centre. From this point on, the waterfront curves northwards.

The coastal road of the town.

A pier to the right, jutting out like a tongue into the harbour, has all the coloured boats gathered around it. A little road going upwards to the left, all stairs, leads to **Tobazis' mansion**, now the property of the School of Fine Arts of the Polytechnic University of Athens. Behind its elegant outer door is a veranda with arches, and the view over the sea from here is fantastic. An even better view can be had from the steep hill with the little church of Ayios Athanasios, from where you can marvel at the whole of the town of Hydra and the surrounding area.

The statue of Pavlos Kountouriotis in the square that has been named after him.

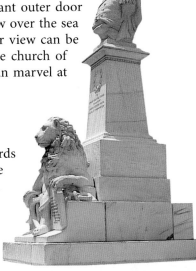

In order to continue the tour of the island, the visitor must return to the coastal road and proceed towards the port exit. To the left, a little before the breakwater, yet another **mansion**, that of **Oikonomos**, dominates the coastal road , and nearby are the **mansions** of **Voulgaris** and **Votsis**.

Periptero
Avlaki
Kaminia

Past the breakwater, the road begins to climb uphill, continuing alongside a rocky road. The first cafeteria which we encounter is built upon the rocks above the crystal-clear blue sea. Its tables are laid out in front. A few metres further up and the road leads to what is perhaps the most beautiful spot on Hydra, the **Periptero.**

This is where the west cannon station is located, and below is the famous **Spilia**, or cave, where all the cosmopolitan youth, and not only, gather for their swim. There are a few pine trees on a wide stretch of the road, at the edge of the base of the rocks and comes upwards, creating a parapet. At every five metres along the parapet a heavy cannon is pointed towards the sea. These are the same cannons, in the same positions, which protected the port during the years of the Revolution.

Below on the rocks, there is a cave in the sea and a rocky islet a little further beyond. Many people gather on the rocks here to enjoy the warm sun, whilst others swim in the sea, enjoying the crystal-clear waters. The parapet proceeds even further along,

1. The beach of Spilia.
2. The crystal-clear blue sea at Periptero.

1

and along with it the cannons. Now there is another cafeteria, larger than the first. The tables here are situated in among the cannons, whilst a canopy hangs overhead to protect the customers from the sun. A staircase leads down to the rocks,

where people are sunbathing and swimming. The sea water at this point takes on an unbe-lievable colour. A blue indigo, mixed in the shallower areas with emerald and green. This location is famous not only for its great beach, but also for its beautiful sunset.

To the left of the road there is a small pine tree forest, in the midst of which stands the beautiful **mansion of Pavlos Kountouriotis**. Behind it is the tall rocky hill of the Myli, with a row

of ruined old mills. The last mill, at the peak, is at the same height as the church of Ayios Athanasios on the hill further to the south. The view from up here is sensational, but the footpath is even more steep than that leading up to Ayios Athanasios.

From Periptero, the road conti-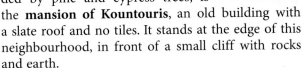nues towards the pretty neighbourhood of **Avlaki**, built on a steep slope of this hill and looking over the sea to the Peloponnesian coast opposite from high above.

Amongst the houses here, surrounded by pine and cypress trees, is the **mansion of Kountouris**, an old building with a slate roof and no tiles. It stands at the edge of this neighbourhood, in front of a small cliff with rocks and earth.

1. The mansion of Pavlos Kountouriotis.
2. Kaminia.
3. The neighbourhood of Avlaki. Bountouris' mansion can be seen on the right.

After Avlaki, the road continues towards the **Kaminia** (Mikro Kamini and Megalo Kamini), the most charming corner on the whole of Hydra. This is a little harbour with dark brown sands located in among two small, rocky hills. The hills are full of old and new houses, and among them are two tavernas on the two edges of the beach. The first taverna is built at a slight rise, and the other has a yellow and red

Kaminia, the most picturesque corner of Hydra.

wall in front of the mole, at which the 'sea taxis' and other small craft dock. The harbour is surrounded by two little breakwaters. Many little boats are moored in behind the breakwaters and in front of the beach, whilst some have even been dragged up onto the sands. All these features together compose a wonderful picture, which is surely an inspiration for all artists, and especially painters.

# of Hydra

View of the town of Hydra with the church of the Ypapanti and the mansion of Kountouriotis.

**Tour
of the town**

After the tour of the port and the walk from Periptero to Kaminia, the visitor can now get to know the inside of the town. The best way to do this is to start at Lignos Street, which is on the right of the Monastiri, turning right a little further down to visit the historic **house of Lazaros Kountouriotis**.

This is now an annex of the National Historical Museum in Athens.

Lazaros Kountouriotis was an important historical figure during the Struggle of 1821. His house was built at the end of the 18th century and is a characteristic example of traditional Hydraiot architecture.

Many important decisions and negotiations for the 1821 War of Independence were made in this house, and it played host to many leading figures of the period.

*1. The mansion of Kountouriotis, today a museum.
2. The traditional pharmacy of Rafalias.*

In its halls today, one can see old island furniture next to console tables and buffets of the same period which the captains brought back with them from abroad, old English and Italian dinner sets, the personal items of Pavlos Kountouriotis, bronze kitchen equipment, baking trays, the bronze bust of Andreas Miaoulis, etc.

The basement of the mansion has a permanent exhibition of paintings by Pericles and Constantine Vyzantios.

On the first floor of this mansion are exhibited, amongst other things, representative works of modern Greek art (18th-19th century) and the traditional costumes of the three main seafaring islands, Hydra, Spetses and Psara.

A guide to the Historic House of Lazaros Kountouriotis (Greek and English) is available in the Museum Shop. One can also find here posters, postcards, publications of the Historical and Ethnological Society. Historical souvenirs are available in the Museum Shop as well.

2

Next to the mansion of Pavlos Kountouriotis is the **church of the Ypapanti** (the All-Holy Virgin), which has a beautiful wood-carved iconostasis. From here, continuing in an eastwards direction among the pretty lanes, we will come to a small square. An old, but excellently-preserved, one-storey building behind the square catches our attention. This is the traditional **pharmacy of Rafalias** which, as a sign on one side says, was founded in 1890! It is a white building, with yellow door and window frames and plaster railings on the parapet of its roof, on top of which two flags fly, the Greek flag and the flag of the European Union. If it is impressive from the outside, then its inside is even more impressive. Nothing has changed inside since the 110 years that have passed since it was founded.

The wooden shelves with the porcelain jars, the drawers with the white-enamel labels, on which the contents are written in black, Latin characters, even the pharmacist's little desk with the old 'accurate' scales set at the edge.

Miaoulis Street, the main road of Hydra, is only a short distance from this pharmacy, where it seems as though time has stopped since 1890. This is the road which leads into the town and terminates at **Kala Pigadia** (Good Wells), one of the oldest and prettiest neighbourhoods of Hydra. The name comes from two wells which are located there. Their parapets are whitened and are covered with a conical iron sheet that has been painted grey. Both are on a raised le-

vel, as the land rises here, which can be reached by climbing up six stone steps. These wells, which are over 200 years old, supply the residents of the old town with water.

The ascending road above Kala Pigadia leads up the hill of **Kiafas**, where Hydra's oldest quarter is built.

1. Kala Pigadia.
2. The neighbourhood of Kiafas.

The neighbourhood of Kiafas with Ayios Konstantinos the Hydraiot.

The beautiful church of **Ayios Konstantinos the Hydraiot** stands tall almost at the top of the hill, at the point where the Saint was martyred. It celebrates its feast day on 14 November, when there is a festival. There is another church in Kiafas which is considered to be one of the oldest in the whole island. This is Ai-Yiannis, with its wonderful wall paintings.

The footpath which leads up to the monasteries of Profitis Ilias and Ayia Evpraxia starts at Kiafas. There is an asphalt-surfaced road for the monastery at Kala Pigadia, but this covers only a section of the route. The rest of it is made along a wide footpath, most of which passes through a thick pine forest.

The mountain in front of the monasteries is bare, and the walker therefore has a chance to admire the wonderful view. Before him is the thick pine forest and down below is the port of Hydra.

The white line of foam left behind by a speedboat can be seen floating on the blue sea, whilst the Peloponnesian coast opposite can be discerned.

The pathway, which just before had quite a few bends as it clambered upwards, suddenly becomes a never-ending stone stairway leading up in a straight path to the entrance of the **Monastery of the Profitis Ilias.** After a strenuous ascent, the grand entrance to the monastery, with the dome above the door and its gold wall painting, begins to stand out. I do not

The Monastery of Profitis Ilias.

know why, but this last section of the road brings to mind a painting of a stairway shaped by the Houris of Paradise, a never-ending staircase which leads up into the sky where it becomes lost in its white light.

The visitors to the Monastery are most welcome, and are given a tour around it by one of the monks. The forecourt around the cathedral church and the monks' cells is huge. A cell in the north-west corner of the Monastery immediately grabs our attention.

This is where Theodoros Kolokotronis, commander-in-chief of the Revolution of 1821, was gaoled for four months in that same year by his own fellow fighters. What injustice, what great destruction division can wreak!

The monastery, built at a height of 500 metres, was founded in 1815, by the monk Hieromonachos, who came to the island in 1813. The Monastery's library has important holdings.

Near the Monastery of Profitis Ilias is the **Convent of Ayia Evpraxia**, the female Saint of Good Acts. It was founded in 1821 and was known for the nuns' handicrafts. Today it has only one nun. Mountain climbers can ascend to the top of Mt Eros from the Monasteries. At 588 metres, this is the tallest mountain on Hydra and lies further to the south-west.

To the east of Hydra town, high up on the mountain, stands the **Convent of Agia Matrona**, which was built in around 1865.

A short distance further east is the **Monastery of Agia Triada**, which is today abandoned. Built in 1704, it looks over Cape Mantraki.

1. The cell in which Kolokotronis was imprisoned in the Monastery of Profitis Ilias.
2. The Monastery of Ayia Evpraxia.

The Convent of Agios Nikolaos, with the wall paintings:
a) Panagia Hodegitria,
b) Agios Nikolaos.

Further south and looking over the cape of Limnionizas is the 17th-century **Convent of Agios Nikolaos**.

On the eastern edge of the island is the **Convent of Zourvas**, one of the most important on the island,

with a wonderful view over the Sea. It takes 3 1/2 hours to reach overland, whilst if you go by boat the ascent only takes another 45 minutes. As for the **Monastery of the Koimisi tis Theotokou**, we have already discussed this in the section on the port of Hydra.

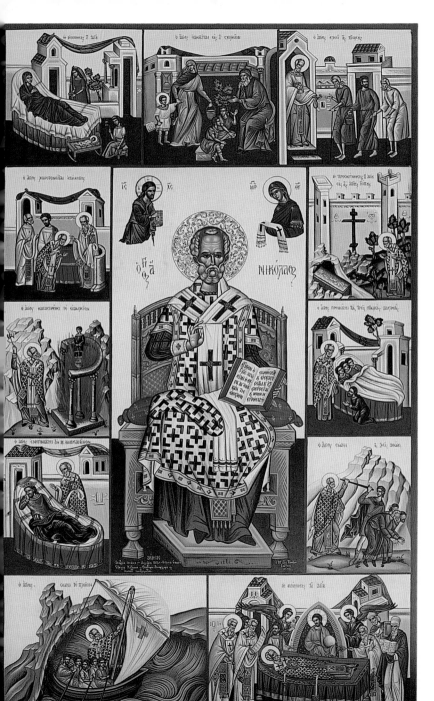

Tour of

The tour of the island gives the visitor the opportunity to see not only the popular beaches, but also the other ones, those which are as equally delightful yet, because they are further from the port of Hydra, there might be only one swimmer in their waters.

This tour, which is made by the 'sea taxis,' as they are known, can commence in a westerly direction, where there is more of interest. The greatest disadvantage of these speedboats is their speed, which means that you do not really get a chance to pro-

The small islet of Limnioniza, is surrounded by the magnificent colours of the sea.

the island

perly enjoy the areas that you will pass. Another disadvantage is that they travel at a distance from the coasts that you wish to see. Both these disadvantages can be overcome by asking the driver to draw up close at any beach you wish to see and even to stop at some of these for a while. But, this must be agreed upon before you start.

The speedboat begins, then, from the port of Hydra, goes around the breakwater and proceeds towards Avlaki and pretty Kaminia, which we saw above. The new feature of this route will soon appear. It is **Vlychos**, a coastal settlement, built on the slope of a pretty mountain. A crowd of freshly-whitened little houses is located on a small, rocky hill, which protrudes into the sea, giving the landscape a special charm. Next to this small hill there is an organised beach with brown sand and deckchairs protected from the sun by large, straw umbrellas.

The next beach after Vlychos is **Palamidas**, with a large, old building to the left with a few boats, protected behind a dyke built next to the sea.

The little **church of Ayios Kyprianos** (St Cyprian) just beyond Palamida appears a brilliant white on a deserted beach with rocks and crystal-clear waters.

1

2

1. The coastal village of Vlychos.
2. The beach of Palamidas.

1, 2. The beach and the little church of Ayios Georgios at Bisti. 3. The bay of Molos. 4. Kaoumithi.

1

After Ayios Kyprianos comes **Molos**, as a large beach with a wonderful pine forest running along its whole length. Behind the pines is a steep cliff, and in front of the beach to the left is a walled estate with old, freshly-whitened one-storey houses and a few summer houses.

From Molos a road which cuts through the densest of the island's few pine forests leads to **Episkopi**. There was a settlement in this area in prehistoric times, only a few of the remains of which survive. Today there are a few summer houses.

The speedboat continues the tour of the island, passing next alongside **Kaoumithi**, with the beautiful and verdant slopes which cut suddenly into the sea. Next, we come to the beach of **Ayios Georgios at Bisti**, near the bay of the same name. This beach has crystal-clear waters and is located in between two hills full of pine trees.

The little **church of Ayios Georgios** dominates on the rocks to the left. There is a small forecourt in front of its entrance, which leads to a stone staircase with five or six steps. Practically all the surfaces are white: the church, the parapet in the forecourt, the dry stone wall opposite. Only the door and window frames, the floor of the forecourt, and the tops of the steps are painted blue. From this little church one

2

3

4

can better enjoy a view of this delightful bay. Some boats tied up on the rocks below add their own touch to the charm of the landscape.

After Bitsi and its bay, the direction of our route changes and we begin to travel in an easterly direction. **Ayios Nikolaos**, a pebbly beach, is relatively close by. There is a large gulf at its cove with rocks to the right and a forest further in. The crystal-clear waters and absolute calm invite us in for a swim. Without a doubt, one can swim at Ayios Nikolaos with the certainty that they will be the only one. The only other presence might be a fishing caique resting on the calm waters.

The same is true at the next beach, **Nisiza**, with the rocks to the right, the brown mountain and the vegetation further in. It is said that the port of the ancient settlement of Episkopi was here.

1. *The beach at Nisiza.*
2. *Ayios Nikolaos, a pebbly beach.*

*Vlychos, wih
the freshly-whitened little houses.*

Continuing our course, the landscape becomes more bare, when, suddenly, the **Spilia tis Fokias** - the cave of the seal - appears, followed by the pretty little **church of Ayios Nikolaos Rigas**, just before the cape of the same name. Built on a rise above the brown rocks next to the sea, there are some small unapproachable bays full of rocks to the right and the left. After the pass from the cape of Rigas, the direction has now changed to a northerly one, soon reaching **Limnioniza**, the most interesting beach on this side of the island. The first sight of the rocks at the entrance and the large sandy beach with its crystal-clear waters is enough to take your breath away. The most beautiful thing, however, is the rocky

1. The 'Spilia tis Fokias', the cave of the seal.
2. Limnioniza, the most interesting beach on this side of the island.

1

islet in the centre, with its stunning colours and the sea all around it.

There are only a few people here, those who have come by caique or speedboat. There are also some, only a few of course, who have come here from Hydra town by foot, walking for two hours in order to enjoy this beautiful beach. Above Limnioniza, at a distance from it, is the **Convent of Ayios Nikolaos**.

In order to continue our little journey we must pass the cape of Zourva, the most easterly point of the island. The Monastery of Zourva soon appears, the most isolated of all on the island, at a distance of three and a half hours from Hydra town. Unless you come by boat, in which case you can moor beneath the Monastery and then walk for 45 minutes to reach it.

1. 2. The pier and the little port at Mantraki.
3. The crystal-clear waters at Limnioniza beach.

1

The tour of the island will end with a visit to **Mantraki**, also known as Miramare, which is 20 minutes from the port of Hydra, or 5 minutes if you take one of the regular speedboat connections.

This was the military port of the Hydraiots during the years of the War of Independence. The bay which we find ourselves in is surrounded by bare and rocky mountains, with beautiful sands at its cove. The tourist complex of Miramare is here. Thanks to its organised beach, it has much to offer visitors for an enjoyable swim and also the chance

2

to indulge in some water sports. Next to the cafe and restaurant is the landing-stage for the boats which come and go from the port of Hydra.

The return journey to Hydra is short, just as the tour of the island with the speedboat was relatively short. Yet, within this brief time, the visitor has had a chance to see the beauties hidden in the island's beaches. He or she will return from this experience full of satisfaction. A satisfaction which leads to one particular desire: to come again.

ISLANDS A

Aegina

Aegina has an area of 84 square kilometres
and is only 17.5 nautical miles from Piraeus Port.
It is an ideal place for short breaks away from Athens.
The churches with their glass domes,
the picturesque narrow alleys,
Angistri and the significant historical monuments
such as the Aphea Temple will win anyone over.

ᴐᴜɴᴅ HYDRA

Aegina

**Things to see in the town
and in the port of Aegina:**
- The church of Ayios Nikolaos
  Thalassinos.
- The mansion of Voyiatzis.
- The traditional carriages.
- The mansion of Kanaris.
- The church of Panayitsa.
- The Folk Museum.
- The tower of Markellos
- The house of Capodistrias.
- The Metropolitan church.
- The Monastery of Faberomenis.
- The church of Ayii Theodorii
  (Beutiful Church).
- The archaeological site
  and the museum of Kolona.
- The Orphanage.
- The house of Kazantzakis.
- The Kapralos Museum.
- The tower of Zaimis.

Aegina

Things to see in the island of Aegina:
- The church of Ayios Nikolaos of Moulou
- The beutiful settling of Kypseli.
- The village of Vathi
- The settling of Souvala,
  the second port of Aegina.
- The monastery of Ayia Aikaterini.
- The little port of Vaia.
- The monastery of Ayios Nektarios.
- The hill of Palaiochora with the
  byzantine churches.
- The monastery of Chysoleontissa.
- Mesagros.
- The temple of Aphaia.
- The village of Pacheia Rachi.
- Ruins from the temple of Zeus Hellanios.
- The holly mountain Oros.
- The little island of Moni.
- The beaches of Ayia Marina and Portes.
- The tourist resort of Marathonas.
- The fishing village of Perdika.
- The organised beach of Aiginitissa.

Things to buy:
- Pistachios.
- Traditional ceramics.

Aegina

Angistri

Things to see in the island of Angistri:
- The church of Ayii Anargyri to the port at Skala.
- The little village of Metochi.
- Mylos, the biggest village of the island.
- The little port of Megalochori.
- The beach at Dragonara.
- Limenaria.
- The islet of Aponisos.
- The beach at Skliri.
- The beach of Halkiada.

Angistri

Salamina

*Salamina is the second largest of the Saronic
islands and the nearest to Athens.
It is covered in pine trees and has beautiful beaches,
especially on the south coast.
The island is best known for the historic
Battle of Salamina, which took place in 480 BC
between the victorious Athenians and the Persians.*

Salamina

Things to see in the island of Salamina:

- The port of Paloukia.
- The nunnery of Faneromeni.
- The beach of Kanakia.
- The beach of Peristeria.
- The bay and the village of Kaki Vigla.
- The port of Kamatero.
- The village of Ambelakia.
- The fishing port of Selinia.

Poros

Poros means passage,
and this is where the name of the island comes from,
since it lies in the south-east of the Saronic Gulf,
opposite the Argolid in the Peloponnese.
Located on the edge of this passage,
built on both sides of a hill, this island society
is a happy one.

Poros

Things to see in the island of Poros:

- The mansion of Kanelopoulos.
- The Archaeological Museum.
- The traditional Roloi.
- The Metropolitan church.
- The mansion of Deimezis.
- The building of Progymnastiria.
- The Kanali.
- The «villa» Galini.

- The little harbour of Agapi.
- The islet of Daskalio.
- The sanctuary of Poseidon.
- The beaches at Askeli and Vagionia.
- The monasery of Zoodochos Pigi
- The islet of Bourtzi.
- The beach of Mikro and Megalo Neorio.

Spetses

Spetses lies at the entrance to the Saronic Gulf. It is the island of Bouboulina, the heroine of the Greek revolution. The many pine trees are a characteristic feature of the island, which in antiquity was known as Pityousa (pitys, yos = pine). There are also charming horse-drawn carriages, beautiful beaches and grand mansions.

Things to see in the island of Spetses :
- The graphic port of Dapia.
- The mansion of Sotiris Anargyrou and the mansion of Boubloulina.
- Spetses' Museum.
- The mansion of Hadjiyiannis Mexis.
- The monastery of Ayios Nikolaos.
- The Old Port (Baltiza).
- The church of Panayia Armata.
- Faros with the statue of gorgon and the Cannon Station.
- The Poseidonio hotel.
- The beaches of Zogeria, Vrellos, Ayii Anargyri, Ayia Marina.
- The neighbourhoud of Kastelli.

Spetses

USEFUL INFORMATION

TRANSPORTATION

Hydra can be reached by ferryboat from Piraeus, on the Piraeus-Aegina-(Methana)-Poros-Hydra-Spetses route. Information: Piraeus Port Authority, tel. 210 4593123, 210 4124585. You can shorten the journey time by taking the hydrofoil from Piraeus (from Akti Miaouli or Zea). Information: Hellas Flying Dolphins, tel. 210 4199200 and Saronic Dolphins, tel. 210 4224777. Journey time lasts from 1 to 3 hours and 20 minutes, depending on the type of vessel.

You can also drive as far as Hermione (3 1/2 hours from Athens) and then take the sea taxi to Hydra.

The use of private cars as well as local buses is prohibited throughout the whole island.

Transport on the island is done by sea taxi, the friendly donkeys and, of course, by foot.

Trails
(Mountain Climbing - Walking)
Hydra is perfect for this activity. The course along the west coast (towards either Mandraki or Kaminia, Vlycho and further) is very enjoyable. The walk required to reach some parts of the island, in particular the monasteries from which the view is spectacular, is also enjoyable.

Mountain climbing allows the visitor to explore Hydra's flora and fauna, to walk through the pine forests and over the mountain slopes filled with wild flowers, such as cyclamens and rare spentzes, and to spot birds such as thrushes, partridges and quails, as well as wild.

There are 10 footpaths from Hydra town to:
1. Kastraki - Kastro
2. Agios Nikolaos
3. Agia Matronis Convent -
   Agia Triada Monastery
4. Hounta Riga
5. Zourvas Convent
6. Profitis Ilias Monastery - Eros
7. Vlycho - Palamida
8. Episkopi - Nisiza
9. Episkopi - Zogeri
10. Agios Mamas - Klimaki

USEFUL TELEPHONE NUMBERS

Area code 22980
Hospital 53150-1
Rural Doctor 52420
Pharmacy 52059,53260
Police 53360
Tourist Police 52205
Port authority 52279
Municipality 52279
Sea taxis 53690
Spetses Museum and Historical Archive 52355
Melina Mercuri
Art and Concert Hall 52955, 53782
Alpha Bank 54053,53141
Emporiki Bank 52041, 53397
National Bank 52578,52986

On Hydra there are many hotels and rented rooms.

BRATSERA	Hydra	A	53971
MIRANDA	Hydra	A	52230
ORLOF	Hydra	A	52564
ANGELICA	Hydra	B	53202
ARES	Hydra	B	53002
GRECO	Hydra	B	53200
HYDROUSA	Hydra	B	52217
LETO	Hydra	B	53385
MIRAMARE	Mandraki	B	52300
MISTRAL	Hydra	B	52509
SIDRA	Hydra	B	53401
AMARYLLIS	Hydra	C	52249
DELFINI	Hydra	C	52082
IPPOCABOS	Hydra	C	53453
NEFELI	Hydra	C	53297
YDRA	Hydra	C	52102
ARGO	Hydra	D	52452
DINA	Hydra	D	52248
SOFIA	Hydra	D	52213

INDEX

Texts: YIANNIS DESYPRIS
Text editor: DAPHNE CHRISTOU
The texts regarding the leaders of the Geek War of Independence
come from the Greek Parliament internet site.
Art editor: EVI DAMIRI
Photographs: Archive M. TOUBIS S.A., YIANNIS DESYPRIS

Production - Printing: M. TOUBIS S.A.